Actions Leading
YOU
To Success

by Bill Kent

Published by Perspicacious Studios, Kings Mills, OH 45034
Contact: Wkent1951@mail.com

Library of Congress Control Number 2020920847
Version 10262020

International Standard Book Number - 978-0-9908304-9-8 (Hardback)

~ Dedicated to anyone wishing to be successful as an employee in any company ~

Acknowledgements

I wish to thank my two special friends for the assistance in writing this book. Through the long and winding road of writing and compiling this work, their encouragement and guidance resulted in a book of which I have always dreamed. This project could not have been done without them.

Preface

I have been blessed with a wonderful career which has taken me down many paths in life's journey.

At times difficult. At time heart wrenching. I have learned so much.

My key principles for success are included within this book. They have worked for me and I sincerely hope they work for you.

And always remember, there is only one rule of corporate survival. KEEP YOUR BOSS'S BOSS, OFF YOUR BOSS'S BACK.

About the Author

Bill Kent serves as the Vice President, Corporate Relations for PK USA, Inc. which is located in Shelbyville, IN. His responsibilities include Human Resources / Safety, Insurance Administration, Environmental Compliance, Information Services Technology. Kent also acts as chief spokesperson for the corporation.

The book is was written based upon Kent's business experiences and serves as his guide to continued success in an automotive market which is constantly changing. The principles contain herein have served him well and he hopes they provide guidance to the reader.

Contents

I. Do Not Worship False Gods

II. Know Your Profession

III. Develop Your Own Style

IV. Put Your Personal Life In Order

V. Know Your Weaknesses

VI. Know Your Strengths

VII. Power and Fear

VIII. Adversaries and Supporters

IX. Network

X. Learn To Delegate

XI. Deliver Quality Service

XII. Learn To Keep Your Mouth Shut

I

Do Not Worship False Gods

Keep your boss's boss off your boss's back.

-    Unknown

This is the first rule of corporate survival.

Follow this rule and you will always be successful.

Remain loyal to your boss and to the company.

- Unknown

The importance of loyalty transcends

every language and cultural difference.

Support your boss's
final decisions, even if you
believe they are wrong.

- Unknown

Never embarrass your boss or let them embarrass themselves.

Provide guidance in making the right decision.

Establish a reputation
for rock hard,
100 % loyalty.

-    Unknown

Every boss wants a loyal employee

and has every right to demand it.

Failure to be loyal creates a haunted career.

- Unknown

And it will haunt you wherever you go
and for whomever you work.

Invest in your future with loyalty as it will pay dividends long term.

-   Unknown

And the dividends will pay handsomely with interest.

II

Know Your Profession

Your career is what you do, not who you are.

- Unknown

Control your career and do not let your career control you.

- Unknown

Take the initiative instead of letting it happen.

Learn your profession early in your career.

- Unknown

Remember you are always learning

but you need to start early.

Capitalize on your advantages or you are at a disadvantage.

Always use your advantages to advance your position.

Put your knowledge to work to become and be known as an expert.

- Unknown

Become an expert in non-traditional roles.

For a 20-year career, make certain you have 20 years of experience, not 1-year experience twenty times over.

-   Unknown

Push your experience into areas outside your comfort factor. It will make you grow.

Shape your entire life to form your business success by linking your activities to your profession.

- Unknown

Use your outside of work activities
to help you grow professionally.

Help others in your company learn their profession. Be a mentor.

- Unknown

It is the right thing to do and others will owe you a favor when you need one.

Discover a job you enjoy doing and you will never have to work a day in your life.

-    Mark Twain

I have worked for the same company

for over 24 years and it is still fun.

If you are thinking about quitting, either do it or forget it.

- Unknown

These are your only two options.

Have Your "I Quit" Money Banked

You need one year banked.

Never quit your job before having another.

If you don't have a job; you don't have money.

Never go down with a sinking ship. Being associated with a failed business is never a positive.

- Unknown

If you are on a sinking ship, you better wear a life preserver. If you work for a company which is a "loser"; then you become a "loser".

III

Develop Your Own Style

Develop your own style,
one that suits you as a
complete person.

- Unknown

Your style should make you approachable.

You should always be willing to assist others.

-    Unknown

And those who assist you
need to be thanked and rewarded.

Be open. Allow people to know and help you.

- Unknown

Anticipate the worst and take action to mitigate the risk.

Learn to always think through an issue

before acting on it.

It's not the hours you put in, but what you put into the hours that count.

- Sam Ewing

You will be appreciated for your achievements,

not your hours at work.

Be an individual that is always fair, ethical, and moral. You will earn trust and be respected.

Never cheat. Never steal. Never destroy.

Remember that the time is always right to do right.

- Martin Luther King Jr.

Doing the right thing is always the best course of action.

- Martin Luther King Jr

Always portray confidence, even when in doubt.

Confidence is contagious. When you are confident, others
will be confident in you.
Sometimes hard to do but always must be done.

Remember that though it is nice to be important; it is more important to be nice.

- John Templeton

People want to know and respect nice people.

Always treat everyone with dignity and respect. It will pay dividends. You never know who your next boss may be.

Being known as a nice person is a good thing.
You can still be firm but fair.

IV

Put Your Personal Life
In Order

When at work,
focus on work.

-    Unknown

This is why you are being paid.

A personal crisis does not mean it is a company crisis.

-    Unknown

A personal crisis can make you fall off the ladder of success. Don't be preoccupied with a personal crisis when climbing the ladder of success.

If you let it, a personal crisis can affect and possibly destroy your career. And frankly, no one cares that you have personal issues.

It sometimes takes two to climb the career ladder. Support each other in this activity.

You are better as a team.

V

Know Your Weaknesses

Recognize the things you cannot do well.

-   Unknown

Find others to do those things you cannot do well until you learn to master them.

- Unknown

Surround yourself with people

who complement your weaknesses.

Learn from these people. It will only make you stronger.

- Richard Branson

VI

Know Your Strengths

Recognize your abilities and continuously develop those skills.

- Unknown

Always learn from those who are smarter than you.

Do the things you do not like first and learn to do them well so you can move on to do the things you enjoy doing.

- Unknown

Your career will be much more enjoyable.

Make your weaknesses your strengths.

- Unknown

You will become a well-rounded employee.

Become known as the "go to" person for difficult or impossible assignments. Then fix the problem quickly.

This principle is high on my list. Always volunteer to handle the impossible assignments. Your value to the company will only rise in the eyes of your boss.

VII

Power and Fear

There is no need to always use your power in order to be powerful.

My requests are handled quickly by subordinates.

Only use the power needed to accomplish the task.

- Unknown

Use power in a manner that is not destructive.

Being known as a powerful person is a good thing.

Temper power with wisdom and humility.

-   Unknown

Never demand; always ask for cooperation and assistance. With this approach you will always get that for which you have asked. Thank those who cooperate.

If you are not at the dinner table, you are part of the menu.

- HR Magazine

You need to be a strategic partner in the business.

Put your enemies on the roof. Just do not let them jump.

-    Unknown

You will always be remembered for how you treat those who oppose you.

VIII

Adversaries and Supporters

Office politics is a reality.
Master this art and be a
politician. Otherwise you
fail.

In a multi-cultural environment, the ability to master

politics is even more important.

Keep your friends close
but your enemies closer.

- Michael Corleone

Always love your enemies, it will confuse them.

- Sermon

Treat your enemies with dignity and respect. It will become difficult for them to attack you.

If your enemies want to hang themselves, make sure they have enough rope.

And make sure your colleagues
know who gave them the rope.

Remain united against your enemies. Strength is in numbers. Use your network to support your causes.

Attack your enemies on many fronts. Continue attacking to keep them unbalanced.

Divide your enemies among themselves. They will fight and destroy each other.

I have used this principle especially when conducting business. It has worked; for many times the snakes will eat their young.

If attacked, remain calm.
If you become emotional,
you are not in control and
cannot respond.

And when your enemies become emotional you know

you have won.

Never forgive those who do you wrong.

It is personal.

Defeated enemies must be treated with respect and dignity.

For that action you will remembered.

Your actions will build respect among the workforce.

The only reliable allies are those who benefit from your success.

Those who support you need to be rewarded. Never forget those who have come to your aid.

IX

Network

Do favors for people to form a network of people who "owe you"

-    Unknown

Establish and use your network because your network

will use you.

Always be willing to cooperate and assist.

- Unknown

Be a team player.

Never prejudge a contact.

- Unknown

Never assume you know what a contact needs or wants.

X

Learn to Delegate

Be an expert at delegating, which means you must pick the right people and trust them to do the right thing.

- Unknown

Let your team manage its own area of responsibility knowing that on occasion mistakes will be made.

Teams will learn from their mistakes.

XI

Deliver Quality Service

Every person is either your supplier or your customer.

Provide the absolute best service to both internal and external customers. You need to be known for your excellent customer relations.

- Tom Peters

Remember your customer is always right especially when your customer is wrong.

Your customer pays your bills and deserves your loyalty and respect.

Always keep your customers informed and look out for their best interests.

Never betray your customer. Always be loyal. Remember, the best way to get new customers is through referrals by your current customers.

XII

Learn to Keep Your Mouth Shut

Do not gossip, do not talk about your plans, make sure you play your cards close to your vest.

- Unknown

Keep confidential matters confidential.

Simply put, shut up.

Learn to keep quiet and look wise.

- Unknown

It is sometimes best to keep your thoughts to yourself.

It is still a principle I need to improve on myself.

Never let your enemies know what you are thinking.
Information is power.

Keep your enemies guessing.